OUT OF THE ORDINARY

For Connie,
One of the most compassionate
& spiritual leaders I know.
With much gratitude & love,
Maria

Out of the Ordinary

COLLECTED POEMS

Marcia Barthelow

PORT STANLEY PRESS
2015

Port Stanley Press
Lopez Island, WA 98261

Copyright @ 2015 by Marcia Barthelow
All rights reserved
ISBN – 13: 978-1507737002

For my mother, Rose Macartney Babson

CONTENTS

Dream Babies   1

#handsupdontshoot   2

Snow Geese   3

Imperfection   4

The Angry Ones   6

Like A Bird On The Wire   9

Call and Response   10

Corinthian's Contusions   11

Winter Storm   12

My Mother's Passing   13

The Mystery of Not Knowing   14

You Know So Well   15

A Case for Love   16

Perseid Showers: Babies of the Dark Night   20

Love the Undiscovered   21

One Night   22

Protest   23

In the Aftermath   24

Your Life   25

The Beat-me-Ups   26

A Father's Dream   34

Remembrance of Things Past   35

What Lies Beneath   36

Stone Rolled From the Sepulcher   37

No Submission   38

Hope   40

Dreamworld   41

Aspiration of Angels   42

Wildflowers in February   44

"I speak from the world of beyond,
out of the ordinary."
~~Rumi

OUT OF THE ORDINARY

Dream Babies

Do not let them die,
    those fragile dream babies.

Feed them on your hospiced hopes;
    your sacred skeptics.

Swaddle their broken hearts with
    blankets of persistent
        attention and patient practice.

Let them breathe of your
    aching hungers as they suckle

on memories of
    cratered connections, forge

new and vital bonds,
    mirror the rhythmic pulse

        – the open,
            close,
                open –

        of your hallowed heart.

#handsupdontshoot

Incensed
can't breathe,
my own denial
brings me to my knees.

Tears of rage,
tears of grief,
they think they walk on water,
is that what they believe?

Snow Geese

You have crested these mountains,
entered this verdant valley,
one-hundred times or more.

Still, the snow geese startle,
white psalmists in the sky.

Imperfection
(with gratitude to Mary Oliver)

You do not have to be perfect.
You do not need to be a star-shiner
polishing your imperfect acts in hope of being chosen
to herald the Nativity.
All you need is to love
all of who you are:
the longings and the half-misses,
the scattered thoughts and the focused passions.

You who believe in the greatness of others
but not your own;
who fear burning out
before you have made your mark,
walk out into the night-time air
and look closely at Orion; the Pleiades:
constellated stars aligned in space,
burning with brilliance,
never altering their position,
though the spinning world will make it seem

as if they are drifting away,
slowly disappearing from
your sight. You out there who deny
your inherent always-was-enough-ness,

go out, again, night after night,
cloudy or starlit, and greet the galaxies
without your star-shiner's cloth.

You who are powerless
to dull or brighten that darkened sky,
go out and receive your gifts:
trajectory and surrender.

And when you come to the edge
of your evening, will you have seen how the darkness
holds the light?
Will you have welcomed your
one, small, meteoric life?

The Angry Ones

They live outside, secretly longing
to be invited in. Open your door to them,
but do not require that they enter.
Instead, return to your kitchen.
Set your table but do not call them
in for dinner. Allow them to pace awhile
outside, even to run through your roses,
ripping them from their roots,
fingertips bleeding as they
tear them apart
petal by petal, shouting
No, when they really mean Yes.

If you are patient,
they will join you at their own pace,
drawn by the aroma
of your freshly-baked bread,
the promise of warmth and sustenance.
Though they are children, all of them,
muddy and riled,
wild and unkempt,
do not force them to wash before
sitting down to eat.
Remember, they have been shamed
and dishonored, ridiculed and lied to;
rejected, misread,

abandoned,
not chosen,
forced to do that
which they would not do.

They have forgotten their manners.
They have forgotten where it is they belong.
Do not try to teach them, do not try
to convince them of their worth,
that the meal has been prepared for them.
They may be afraid at first even to sit,
eyeing with uncertainty
the steaming bowls of soup,
the thick bread and rich butter for spreading.
If they do take a chair,
they may place it as far away
from you as possible.
Allow them any table edge they choose;
ignore how their feet jiggle
so fiercely that your floor vibrates;
no one will perish, do not ask them to stop.

If they slam their spoons
against your plates,
do not scold them,
otherwise, you will become
the thing they fear the most,
you will become just like them:
tight and distrustful.

Remember,
this time they have hurt no one:
they have not hurt you,
they have not hurt each other,
they have not hurt themselves.
Even if the plates are shattered,
unusable, ruined,
just clear away the shards,
sweep them into the trash,
laugh out loud and
bring new plates to be filled,
not when you finally force these
young ones to eat,
but whenever it happens
that they are ready,
whenever they choose
to settle in,
to reach out and serve themselves.

Like A Bird On The Wire

The elephant strode into the room
round crystal weights shifting
from piano to coffee table,
pencils scribbling on walls,
the sound of glass breaking
striking notice that
things
were
no longer.

I fell into a dream of you,
could not replace the shingles
that blew off our roof
with your anger.
Yesterday,
I remembered
how tall you were;
how small the trees became,
the way the robins still sang.

Call and Response

In my dream you were lost.
Strange songbirds serenading
your stumbling attempts
to make your way through
a dense cobweb maze.

Your name burned in my chest,
erupted from my throat
like the sharp explosive *chink*
of the white-throated sparrow.

I woke into the echo
of that loud, foreign cry
trembling with the unfinished scene;
breezes riffling the curtains,
shadows spinning
across the white bedroom wall.

Corinthian's Contusions

Blind, frightened power
pursuing imagined threats
dim-lit mirrors fail

Winter Storm

The wind has offered
its forgiveness.
From beyond the
glaciated peaks,
it shifts and swirls
as if there were so many
possibilities
it can not be imprisoned
by attaching to just one.
Still the rain comes.
Torn from mother clouds,
it slashes rivulets of
altered reflections
across half-opened windows,
drowns newly seeded fields
with its persistence.

My Mother's Passing

What if you were a hummingbird,
I were the moon?
We'd spend every hour
in love with life's croon.

You'd flit over hilltops
those cliffs above seas
your wing beats would whisper
in sweet harmonies,

while beams from my inner world
sang to the sands,
I'd learn of those secrets
that o'er your life spanned

we'd share lyrics, and love notes
and twisted good-byes
would that I could bend down to you,
or you could rise.

The Mystery of Not Knowing

Who knew that the feast of Stephen
was a day, and not a place
where king and page trod
seeking yonder peasant.
That Christmas, snuggled up on the floor
beneath the carefully icicled tree,
I peeked out from beneath my mother's
white, chenille bedspread (the one
we got to use when we were sick) to listen
to carolers at the front door, my thumb worrying
the special corner hole.

I closed my five-year-old eyes,
scanning my own snowy fields
of memory, seeking my brother
of the same name who weeks before
had entered the dark, hospital hallway
and not returned.
I imagined a field being named for him,
my footsteps walking in the dinted snow
where his had been:
me, hoping to catch up.

You Know So Well

You know so well that fear
    of being left behind, unseen.

And call to you the truth that no one survives;
    that everyone you love will leave.

But have you forgotten
    that constant dragonfly stream?

How first you feared,
    then loved their presence?

The outlaw who landed on your shirt,
    wingtips glittering in the sun?

A Case for Love

In the end you will be asked,
Did you pursue what stirs you most?
Not if you've saved more than enough
or travelled coast to coast.

Sometimes, for me, it's hard to find
what flutters deep within,
I have a sense of weariness,
my patience can wear thin.

So *often* when I just can't find
the next step I should take,
I search out places far and wide
in which I have no stake.

I think that other people
will help me find the way:
I ask, and then reject
advice,
it's like I have no say.

I get confused, I cannot think,
my spirits they sink lower.
I eat some ice cream, drink some tea,
seek answers from some knower.

Of one thing I am certain,
though we pretend it isn't so,
only *you* can save your life,
it makes no difference where you go.

Not through the love of others
will you find your heart's desire,
your deepest and felt-senses
will reveal your inner fire.

Listen to your body's rhythms:
harmonics heard in rustling thoughts,
the hum of inner voices,
revealing truths that they have sought.

Like an inner city's rumblings,
is your own internal light,
sirens wailing, heartbeats pulsing
dancers twirling in the night.

You can touch it all, it beckons,
even that which puts up walls;
your world inhales with deepest longing,
unseen inner-pathways call

for your open-hearted tenderness,
not some wisdom from afar;
just the brush of calloused fingertips,
along your jagged scars.

No one upon this earthly path
will ever really know,
what waits for us behind the veil
that's thin and richly flows;

but when your time is finished,
and Love comes to your door,
will you say, I saw you coming,
it was *you* I waited for?

Perhaps you'll greet Love warmly,
as an old, familiar friend,
say, You've been with *me*
my whole damn life,
I wonder where *I've* been?

We won't have candied possum tails
or jubilee regret,
I'm sure our end is not like that,
though I've not been there yet.

One thing I know is while we're here,
each moment we can choose,
to enter fully into life
and all our messy ooze,

or we can keep our distance,
It's not *me*, it's *him*! we'll say.
But then we really have no light
that helps us find our way.

We have one chance to open up,
or perhaps we've lifetimes more,
but it doesn't really matter,
Love is what we're put here for.

If we can look within and feel
the fever and the flow,
we'll solve the mystery of life,
and war and hate won't grow.

Instead we'll find new ways that we
can reach across the chasm,
to try on someone else's shoes
or sense their cytoplasm!

So today, and then tomorrow,
and for all the days to come,
we say, Hurrah! for all we're given,
'cause of us, there's only one!

Perseid Showers:
Babies of the Dark Night

They tumble, twirl,
struggle to survive; streak
across the nighttime sky: dust
returning unto dust.
As we
    — infants ourselves —
lie prone in the galaxy of time,
turn to gaze upward, senses free-falling
with desire, caught in each other's wake;
fingertips touch, and release.

Love the Undiscovered

Do not let your wild horses keep you
from doing whatever it is you love.
If you can find nothing you love to do,
then love the undiscovered.
If the undiscovered only makes you angry,
because you do not know what it is,
love the anger.
If the anger, in its bold, demanding cataclysm
brings you fear, love your fear.

If fear makes you tremble and prance about,
stampedes into your lungs and throat,
threatens to crush every bone in your body,
love the trembling and prancing,
the stampeding and snorting,
the breathless desire to be seen
and discovered, to feel flesh upon flesh;
to be reined in with love.

One Night

One night
you couldn't hear
all that you were called to do,
as you left your burning house.
Muddled by the smoke
and fear of flames,
you forgot, for just a moment,
the angry child still sleeping deep inside.
You scooped up the handicapped one
from the cot beside you,
cuddled her head to your chest
to quiet her whine.
Stumbling, you grabbed her leg braces
and rushed for fresh air,
but somehow failed the one
who most likely dreamed of your demise.
You left her there, all blanketed over,
no doubt still tucked into fetal position,
like those "pill bugs" you tormented
when you yourself were only a child,
poking them here and there until
they curled upon themselves in protection.

Protest

There will come a day
when darkness
will be celebrated as deeply
as the power of the light;
when fear
will no longer suffocate
those of a different heritage.

There will come a day when
all men and women will
come together,
free from watch-dogging the *other;*
free from pursuing
in order not to be pursued;
free from grinding down
the sharp edges of our diversity
through violence and oppression.

There will come a day
when circles,
instead of lines,
will be drawn.

In the Aftermath

Sometimes, it is just living
    into the small graces that gets us through:

raindrops on the window,
    light from a streetlamp in the misty evening,

memories of hands held in love:
    We are who we were meant to be.

Your Life

Can you imagine yourself
like the honeysuckle,
lingering, delicate,
filled with sweet nectar,
always leaning toward release
from your trellis,
your life-blood transported
by curious hummingbirds
who dart from vine to vine?

The Beat-Me-Ups

They beat me up
they really do
these voices say
their points of view,

about how *I*,
(without a brain!),
have made mistakes,
have caused disdain.

I am *not* perfect
cannot track,
they say
so many things I lack:

like honesty, and
vision clear, and
ways to keep
my dear ones near.

They say if *I*
would only *try*,
I'd never lose
I'd never cry.

But that is really
not their fear
they're scared I'll
make you leave me here.

That you will hate me,
or what's worse,
you just won't see me
(or this verse).

They think you have
a true surfeit
of friends,
in fact, they're sure of it.

That you'll decide
way deep within,
I have no worth
They make a din!

They think you hate me,
that you'll pour
your punishment
upon my door.

They say that I'm not
good enough.
"Too soft," they say,
instead of tough.

They fear that
Poof! I will be gone,
no one will ever
hear my song,

or love me up
or stroke my head,
or cuddle *me*
up in my bed.

So what is *I*,
poor soul to do?
except to cling,
eyes closed, to you!

And try my hardest,
yes, to guess,
how I might win
your deep caress,

your smile,
your invite into love,
how can I be
your turtle dove?

It sounds quite silly,
but it's not,
to these poor parts
you're all they've got!

And they are feeling
very sad!
And also very,
very mad.

They want to *be held*
and to hold,
they want the silver
and the gold.

They want the up,
they want the down,
they want the spinning
round and round.

They want it all to be one place,
they think it's not, and so they race
from me to you, and back
to me,

and then to others who they see,
that seem to offer what *you* do:
a love that no one
can undo.

But then it all just starts again
(and feels like this will never end).
They come too close
they stray too far

they wonder who, and where
you are.
These beat-me-ups
the ones who long

the ones who try
to keep me strong,
so I won't need
the likes of you,

but then of course
I always do.
And so it goes
all 'round and 'round,

and all takes place without a sound.
It's inside *me* – this pitter-pat
of: you did this, and
you did that,

this wasn't right,
that wasn't good,
you've let them down
misunderstood,

you'll find yourself alone
they say,
with no one who can
really play.

They're much too young
to understand
a love lives deeper
in our land,

who does not make
us do it right,
who understands
with deep insight;

a love who feels
their pain and grief,
who calms their fears
and brings relief.

They do not know
it's in us all,
a deeper love
that hears our call,

they haven't yet
turned toward their hearts
to understand
we're all a part

we're not alone,
not here or there,
we've all been given
love to share.

And that's enough
for now at least,
they're feeling quite
a bit more peace.

And so I tuck them into bed,
remind them of all that I've said:
how love is patient, love is kind,
love takes their hand, love makes this rhyme.

Love holds them when they're feeling sad,
love lifts them up, love makes them glad.
Deep love is one surprising Yup!
it says, Come on in here and sup

with me, whenever you feel low
or when it's just too far to go
all by yourself, all on your own…
come rest with me, I'm always home.

A Father's Dream

I have lived with nothing
but sixpence and decay,
shouldering unspent boulders
up incandescent hillsides,
only to pause for breath,
ignite delay, become rooted
to the place of uncertainty
and hesitation,
where I hear but do not see
the stone's retreat; the propulsion
backward toward the ever-present call
of descent and return.

Remembrance of Things Past

Sometimes
the nightingale
hovers at the edge
of my wakeful
dream state,
calling me to remember
your voice
in the rustling leaves,
to feel in my own
fluttering heart,
how deeply you
wanted to
(but, alas, could not)
hold me.

What Lies Beneath

Sundays we walk
parasols or rainbows,
puddle splashes
or dry riverbeds;
makes no matter.

Hand in hand
we,
bespeckled with incantations,
imagine our eyes
as little starlight specks
of gratitude
for the opening of
textured tunnels
leading deep
underground.

Stone Rolled From the Sepulcher

Alone on the beach, with the sandpiper scurrying
toward, and then away from, the water's edge,

you imagine another lifetime of earthly lassitude.
But there are the crocuses, warming each other

in purple clusters at the edge of the little garden
by your front gate; and those two robins:

red-bellied, focused, persistently foraging in the tall
lawn-grass, battling each other for the earthworm.

No Submission

I have no intention
of commending my soul
to you
or any of your servants:
not the breath of fire,
the watcher on the tower,
or the keeper
at the gate.

When I go, I shall bring her with me
wrapped in swaddling clothes.
Together, as one, we shall
mount up on wings as eagles,
we shall cross the thin veil
into the land of immaculate plenty.

Wiley conniver that you are,
trying to trick me into believing
your goodness – I know you want me
only for yourself and your
appetites. You think you can
separate us. You think we are
yours for the asking.

Beware the heart of a woman.
Beware the radiant mother of all.
Beware the power of pure love
that can never be divined by one
who seeks only to be loved
and not to be
love.

Hope

If you want me,
when roses are budding,
unfurling from the shy,
cut-back-a-season-ago stems,
and it seems an eternity stands between
then and when-it-will-be-again,
just breathe of their new-birth essence,
let your eyes rest upon the possibilities,
imagine the full-lipped opening.

Dreamworld

In the darkening twilight,
when the stars, like
champagne bubbles,
danced into being,
infusing the night sky with
our effervescence,
I felt your hand,
remembered your body
against mine, laughed
into drunken possibilities.

Aspiration of Angels

I called that they might
feel my pulse,
open the door to my desire,
untangle the twisted vines.

I already know the path,
though that longing for the other
breathes through every pore, constrains
the beating of my heart.

The night air brings with it an ancient cradle,
the wind sings a lullaby;
like a dervish, silver laughter
breaks the stony silence.

I imagine perfumed angels
transcribing the beat of hummingbird wings;
the cobra coils at my feet,
and I weep for the moon.

They hover almost within reach,
whisper my destiny
passed down through
the ages, fleeting as Haiku:

dewdrops shimmering
naked on cherry blossoms
preparing to fall

The angels sing my fragility,
call me by name (from daybreak to dusk,
and through this midnight hour)
to raise my voice in counterpoint.

Unharnessed, my lungs expand,
my heart stretches as we tumble,
twisting into darkness,
the emptiness like a serrated edge between us,
and I fear the light, so white, I cannot sleep.

Wildflowers in February

I did not expect to find wildflowers
in February, any more than I supposed
your face would appear
to me suddenly, confirming my sense
that you weren't quite gone,
that our lives were still linked,
embodied in sisterhood:
twin rainbows spanning the straits
stretching endlessly out before me.

I'd gone down to the point
that morning, just me and my puppy dog,
who bounded through tufted
grass meadows, raced
up mossy rock outcroppings, leaped
over logs and found our familiar footpaths
that twisted and turned,
rose and descended,
always taking their cues from the sea.

Despite disbelief of your presence there with me, (Or
maybe because I still courted that truth) I found
myself searching
for signs on those wild, windswept cliffs
where you and I still walked in my mind.

Just down from the hilltop,
tucked out of the wind, I knelt down
to finger a small, spiny, green thing
(thinking it quite like the way you could be,
bristly and camouflaged there in the moss).
I didn't know the plant's name,
(nor those of the wildflowers
that later would bloom in the meadows).
How would I have taken the time?
Our walks weren't like this: unhurried reflections
on a life and it's meaning.

We usually ran with our dogs,
often just before sunset;
on that last summer evening,
when we'd run out of breath
and relaxed to a walk, our talk
turned to all that we'd do
when our lives finally slowed down:

make that road trip to Mexico, host a poetry slam,
spend all day in our pjs eating nothing but
strawberries and Devonshire cream.

I unzipped my down coat to get air,
suddenly so done with those memories
of you, and turned my back toward the sea,
hating that glitter and shine,
sunlight dancing on stagnant, flat waters
and my ludicrous hope that you'd unfold
in some symbolic mystery,
materialize on that hillside specially for me.

Erasing thoughts of your Brain Masses,
how your body had withered away,
I yanked out that seedling,
filling my mind with the *heet heet heet*
of an eagle's call, and the visceral
memory of our dogs running free
– your seafaring lab; my malamute mutt,
all wildness and untamed energy –
how they'd race into thickets
ignoring our warnings,
(imagined you saying, They doggedly pursued their
unseen prey. Which of course brought the thought
that your tumors
had come the same way).

I hadn't intended to grieve you,
we rarely shared tears you and I,
but those secreted memories
and that little spiked something
still clutched in my palm, blurred up my vision, finally convinced me
your body was gone.

Who knows who then carried your whisper?
Who knows how the wind rose
and ribboned those waters, making pathways
to carry us out to the sea?
Who knows how that granite rock called me,
who blossomed the lone, yellow wildflower
that seemed to appear out of nowhere,
tucked under the stone, its round little blooms
bundled up there at my feet?

ACKNOWELDGEMENTS

I wouldn't have become the person I am, and therefore would not have written *these* poems, without the steadfast love of my husband, Michael, who read and edited my many drafts; and of my daughters, Sarah and Katie, who kept me from slicing and dicing the poems into oblivion.

I would never have transitioned from posting poems on my blog to putting together this book without the support of *so many friends*. You all know who you are!

In addition to all who have read and encouraged and commented and cajoled, I'd like to thank Barbara Barthelow Glazis, who unfalteringly read (and liked or commented on) every poem I ever put in front of the general public; Sarah Barthelow, who created the cover (several iterations, without once commenting on my obsessive disorder), Kelli Buzzard and Lorna Reese who offered the title; and Clare Campbell and Mary Steege, who played chief cheer-leaders and hand-holders throughout.

Last but not least, in memory and in love, I am forever indebted to the members of my Lopez writers' group: Alie Smaalders, Georgie Muska, John Sangster, Kip Greenthal, and Marcia Simpson.

Made in the USA
Charleston, SC
21 February 2015